4/20

— OUTDOOR ADVENTURES —

BOATING

By Patricia Hutchison

SportsZone

An Imprint of Abdo Publishing
abdobooks.com

abdobooks.com

Published by Abdo Publishing, a division of ABDO, PO Box 398166, Minneapolis, Minnesota 55439. Copyright © 2020 by Abdo Consulting Group, Inc. International copyrights reserved in all countries. No part of this book may be reproduced in any form without written permission from the publisher. SportsZone™ is a trademark and logo of Abdo Publishing.

Printed in the United States of America, North Mankato, Minnesota
092019
012020

THIS BOOK CONTAINS RECYCLED MATERIALS

Cover Photo: Collin Quinn Lomax/Shutterstock Images
Interior Photos: Josh Schutz/Shutterstock Images, 5; Hulton Archive/Getty Images, 6; Kuznetcov Konstantin/Shutterstock Images, 8; Rena Schild/Shutterstock Images, 11; Tero Vesalainen/Shutterstock Images, 12; Shutterstock Images, 14, 16, 17, 19, 20 (canoe paddle), 26, 30, 32, 41; Pashkov Andrey/Alamy, 20 (rowing oar); Travis Manley/Shutterstock Images, 20 (kayak paddle); iStockphoto, 20 (rafting paddle), 42; EB Adventure Photography/Shutterstock Images, 22; Fat Camera/iStockphoto, 25, 29; Nicky Rhodes/Shutterstock Images, 35; Apiwich Pudsumran/Shutterstock Images, 36–37; Patricia Dulasi/Shutterstock Images, 38; Jodi Jacobson/Shutterstock Images, 45

Editor: Patrick Donnelly
Series Designer: Colleen McLaren

Library of Congress Control Number: 2019942085

Publisher's Cataloging-in-Publication Data

Names: Hutchison, Patricia, author
Title: Boating / by Patricia Hutchison
Description: Minneapolis, Minnesota : Abdo Publishing, 2020 | Series: Outdoor adventures | Includes online resources and index.
Identifiers: ISBN 9781532190469 (lib. bdg.) | ISBN 9781532176319 (ebook)
Subjects: LCSH: Boats and boating--Juvenile literature. | Recreation boating--Juvenile literature. | Watercraft--Juvenile literature. | Boats--Juvenile literature. | Outdoor recreation --Juvenile literature.
Classification: DDC 797.1--dc23

TABLE OF
CONTENTS

CHAPTER 1
BOATING THEN AND NOW 4

CHAPTER 2
GET EQUIPPED 10

CHAPTER 3
GET MOVING 18

CHAPTER 4
SAFETY TIPS 28

CHAPTER 5
RESPECT THE ENVIRONMENT 40

GLOSSARY 46
MORE INFORMATION 47
ONLINE RESOURCES 47
INDEX 48
ABOUT THE AUTHOR 48

BOATING THEN AND NOW

The raft pushes off from the riverbank and floats peacefully through steep canyons of towering trees. Birds soar quietly above. Suddenly, the boaters hear rushing water—the first set of rapids. The water moves faster. The front of the raft lifts high in the air.

The guide yells, "Keep paddling!" The rafters' hearts pound in their chests. The rubber boat bounces off the rocks like a giant pinball. Cold water crashes over the paddlers' faces as they steer the raft around the obstacles. Then the water is calm again. The rafters' burning muscles get a

White-water rafting can make for an exhilarating day on the river.

Recreational boating dates back to the 1600s in Europe.

well-deserved rest. They catch their breath and smile after a job well done.

The idea of hurtling down a river in a blow-up boat while navigating through rapids, around boulders, and down waterfalls sounds crazy to some people. To others, it's the perfect adventure. Rafting, like all types of boating, takes people to beautiful places that may be otherwise impossible to reach. It brings them closer to nature and to their companions.

NOT JUST FOR THE RICH

Today, it is common to see families and friends taking their boats out for an afternoon on the water. But that wasn't always the case. Boats have been around since prehistoric times. Back then, they were mostly used for work. Indigenous people built canoes for fishing. Greeks and Romans used huge rowboats with hundreds of oars for transportation.

Recreational boating didn't develop until much later. Historians believe that boating for sport began in the 1600s. At that time, it was a pleasure reserved

THE FIRST YACHT CLUBS

As boating became popular, there was no place for boaters to gather. Finally, in the early 1700s, many of the yachtsmen came together to form sailing clubs. Historians disagree as to which club came first. Some think it was the Water Club of the Harbour of Cork in Ireland. Others believe the Neva Yacht Club in Russia was the first.

for royalty and the upper class. They enjoyed grand regattas on the Thames River in England.

Charles II of England is recognized by historians as the first yachtsman. Before he became king in 1660, he spent 10 years in Holland. When he returned home, he was welcomed with a gift of a yacht and crew. King Charles spent much time boating on the Thames. Historians estimate he built as many as 20 yachts during his lifetime.

According to one study, nearly 142 million Americans went boating in 2016. Most of them had yearly incomes of less than $100,000. The average age for a person's first boating experience is 12 years old. Boating for fun has come a long way since its beginning, when it was reserved for only royalty and the rich. Now it's an activity that millions of people can enjoy.

Millions of Americans enjoy spending time on the water each year.

CHAPTER 2

GET EQUIPPED

Boating has its own language, especially when it comes to the parts of the boat. The hull is the body of the boat. This is the part the paddler sits in. The front of the boat is called the bow. The rear is the stern. When looking toward the bow, the left side is the port side. The opposite side is called starboard. Aft is the area toward the stern of the boat. Forward is the area toward the bow.

ROWBOATS

There are many different types of boating. Rowing is done for both recreation and competition. It is common to see people on a lake fishing from a rowboat. Some row for exercise or just to spend a relaxing day on the water. Others join rowing teams

Some athletes participate in competitive crew in college and beyond.

A rowboat's oars are anchored to the boat by oarlocks.

in high school or college. They compete in races on lakes or rivers.

Rowboats used for recreation are pointed at the bow. The hull widens out and is somewhat shallow. Bench seats span the middle, and the stern is usually squared off. They can carry several people, along with picnic baskets and other important gear. However, rowboats are heavy and difficult to move, both in and out of the water.

What makes a boat a rowboat are the oars. These are the paddles that move the boat through the water. A recreational rowboat has one set of oars, about eight feet (2.4 m) long. They are held in place by the oarlocks. These are pieces of metal on the top ridges of the boat. They provide a point for the oars to pivot when the pilot is rowing.

CANOES

Canoes are pointed on both ends. They are narrower and deeper than rowboats. Canoes are light and travel fast. But they are difficult to keep upright in the water. Canoeists use short paddles that are about five feet (1.5 m) long. They provide both steering and propulsion. It is a challenge to paddle a canoe in a straight line. This is because the paddle is used on only one side of the boat at a time.

KAYAKS

Kayaks come in several shapes and sizes. There are two main types. Boaters sit on top of a recreational kayak. Their legs are exposed. Sit-in kayaks are used

Some kayaks are built for one person, while others have two seats.

for touring. Boaters' legs are enclosed. Most carry only one person. But some kayaks have two seats. Both types use double-bladed paddles. The paddle length depends on the height of the boater.

WHITE-WATER RAFTS

White-water rafts can carry up to 12 people. In many cases, a group consists of six to eight people with a guide sitting on the back. The rafts are made of synthetic materials such as rubber or plastic. The material is tough and slides easily over rocks.

Rafts have several air chambers. If one is damaged, air will be left in the others so the boat stays afloat. Most rafts are designed with an upturned nose. Inflatable tubes run across the bottom of the boat where the paddlers sit. These are called thwarts. Rafters use a short, single-blade paddle. It has a T-shaped grip at the top. The guide usually has two paddles. They are longer and are used to steer the raft through the water.

CLASSES OF WHITE-WATER RAFTING

Rafting difficulty is based on how tricky the river is to navigate. Rivers are graded by the International Scale of River Difficulty. There are six classes. Class I is easy. The water moves fast, but there are few obstacles. Class VI rivers are difficult and dangerous. They should be navigated only by experts.

White-water rafts are made of rubber or plastic and are inflated before use.

White-water rafters are smart to carry some equipment. A repair kit will come in handy in case of a blowout. Of course, a good pump will be needed to reinflate the raft. Most rafters wear wetsuits. A wetsuit should be thick enough to keep the boater warm. It could help prevent hypothermia if the raft capsizes and the boaters are left floating in the frigid water.

BASICS FOR ALL WATERCRAFT

If the boat tips, everything will scatter into the water. Gear should be kept in a waterproof pouch. Snacks and fresh water will be protected in a floating cooler. Of course, all boaters should carry basic safety equipment, such as a first aid kit, sunscreen, snacks, and a cell phone or radio.

CHAPTER 3

GET MOVING

Boats move using basic physics. The paddler moves the water in one direction with the oar or paddle. The boat moves the other way. The boaters pull and push a blade through the water. As the boaters paddle faster, the boat goes faster. Many people who know little about boating might think rowing and paddling are the same thing. They might talk about rowing a canoe or call a paddle an oar. However, there are several differences between rowing and paddling. There are also differences between paddling a canoe, a kayak, and a raft.

The biggest difference between rowing and paddling is the tool used to move the boat. Oars are used in rowing. Paddles are used to pilot a canoe,

Different types of boating call for different paddles and strokes.

—TOOLS OF THE TRADE—

Rowing Oar

Canoe Paddle

Kayak Paddle

White-Water
Rafting Paddle

kayak, or raft. Oars move boats in the opposite direction from the way the rower is facing. Paddles move the craft in the direction the paddler is facing. So, rowers go backward, and paddlers move forward. Also, oars are usually longer than paddles.

Oars are attached to a rowboat. Rowers use their legs and arms to push and pull the oars and make the boat move. Two oars are needed—one on each side of the boat to help it move in a straight line. Paddles are held in the boaters' hands. They use their chests and upper bodies to push the blade down into the water.

CANOEING vs. KAYAKING

The biggest difference between canoeing and kayaking is the vessel. Canoes are open, and kayaks have a deck. Canoeists sit higher on the water than kayakers do. Canoes are navigated using a single-bladed paddle. Kayaks require a paddle that's double-bladed. Moving a kayak uses less time between strokes. This makes them go faster than

Canoes have an open top and sit higher in the water than kayaks.

a canoe. Since canoes are usually narrower than kayaks, they are less stable. Often canoeists have to kneel in the boat to keep it balanced.

ROWING A BOAT

Rowing is done using opposite motions. Raising the handles of the oars lowers the blades into the water. Then the rower leans back and pulls the blades straight through the water. The handles are then lowered to raise the blades out of the water as the rower leans forward. This movement is considered one stroke. The boat glides forward, and the stroke will begin again. After some practice, experienced rowers will be able to make smooth strokes. The movement of both oars will be balanced. Opposite motions are also used to steer a rowboat. To turn left, the rower makes strokes using only the right oar. The left oar is used to turn the boat to the right.

If there is more than one rower, each can take an oar. But they must work well together and try to match their strokes. If not, they will end up rowing in circles.

PADDLING A CANOE

Kneeling or sitting in the hull, the canoeist holds the paddle with both hands. One hand is on top, and one is above the blade. The handle is straight up and down. The blade is perpendicular to the side of the boat. A paddler pushes the blade down into the

GETTING A WORKOUT

Rowing and paddling can be strenuous. The trick to minimize tired muscles is to use proper form. Boaters must put the blade of the paddle far enough in to stir the water. Otherwise, they will end up splashing and going almost nowhere. They will have tired muscles without having moved far.

water and pulls it through. As the blade leaves the water, the boater's bottom hand comes up, moving the blade out from the boat. The handle is then parallel with the top of the canoe. Then the paddler repeats the stroke on the other side.

If there is more than one paddler, they work together on opposite sides of the boat. One sits in front and the other in the back. To steer the canoe, the stroke is done only on one side at a time. As in rowing, the right paddle moves the boat left, and vice versa.

PADDLING A KAYAK

Boaters sit in the kayak's seat. They put both hands toward the middle of the double-bladed paddle. Leaning forward, they push one blade down, pull

Hand position is very important when paddling a canoe.

the blade through the water, and then pull up while leaning back. Then they repeat the motion on the other side of the boat with the other blade. Their arms make a figure-eight movement. The blades act like a paddle wheel. With practice, kayakers learn to put the blade in close to the craft. This allows them to grab as much water as possible.

Kayakers need to paddle together in order to move forward in a straight line.

If there are two people on the kayak, they must try to synchronize their motion. If their strokes are off, they will be working against each other. The kayak will end up zigzagging through the water or not going anywhere at all.

WHITE-WATER RAFTING IS UNIQUE

Because white-water rafting is done on a river, the current moves the boat. Rafters need to be more concerned with steering through rapids and around boulders. The safest way to raft is with a group and a guide. An even number of people sit on each side of the raft. They use T-grip paddles. The guide sits in back and helps steer the raft.

When the guide yells "Paddle!" the work begins. People on one side put one hand over the paddle's grip. The other hand grips the shaft. Using their core muscles, they stretch forward and place the paddle in the water at a right angle. They straighten their bodies and pull the paddle through the water, either forward or backward. Then the rafters lift the blades out of the water. Usually, the two front paddlers set the timing. They try to get everyone to work together. The raft moves left or right, depending on which side is paddling. The pace is fast and exhausting. But the experience is thrilling.

CHAPTER 4

SAFETY TIPS

A boat trip can be relaxing or exciting. It can also be dangerous. Water is a force of nature, and boating accidents can cause injury or death. However, following a set of simple safety tips can minimize a boater's risk.

SAFETY EQUIPMENT

All boaters must carry basic safety equipment. First on the list is a personal flotation device (PFD) for each person in the vessel. A PFD is also known as a life jacket. Each person's PFD must fit properly and be approved by the US Coast Guard. There are sizes for both adults and children. Rubber arm floaties or swim rings are not acceptable substitutes.

Life jackets are a must for every person in the boat.

29

Beginners should plan to stay close to shore until they get more comfortable on the water.

PFDs help to keep boaters' heads above water if they go overboard.

A whistle is also an important piece of safety equipment. Blowing a whistle will alert other vessels of your position in the water. Handheld flashlights are useful when boating in misty weather or at night. A basic first aid kit should be on board every boat. Sunscreen can help prevent a blistering sunburn.

PLAN FOR SAFETY

Rowers, canoeists, and kayakers should know their surroundings. Beginners, especially, should choose a calm spot away from wind and waves. Boating near the shoreline is a smart thing to do. There will be less boat traffic. Also, being able to see land can have a calming effect. Boaters who do stray farther should stop every so often to check their bearings and be certain they know how to get back to shore.

Checking the weather forecast is also a smart safety precaution. If storms or high winds are predicted, boaters should schedule their trip for another day. Whenever possible, it is safer to boat with a partner. Even then, boaters should tell someone on shore where they are going and what time they plan to return. If the boaters do not return

Boaters should always check the weather forecast before heading out on the water.

on time, this person can notify others, including authorities if necessary.

Rowers and paddlers need to know water traffic rules. It is important to keep a lookout for other boats. Rowboats and paddleboats do not travel as fast as motorboats. Paddlers should never cross in front of them. The safest thing to do is to wait for the motorboat to pass and then cross astern. Waves created by motorboats are a hazard to paddleboaters. The best way for the navigator to cross is to point the boat directly into the waves. All boaters must pay attention to safety warnings and listen to those in authority.

BRING A SPARE

It's a good idea for recreational navigators to carry a spare set of oars or paddles. Safe boaters also pack a bailing jug with a wide mouth. This can come in handy if their boat springs a leak. They should try to keep the boat flat on the water. It should never be overloaded with equipment

LIGHTNING THREAT

Thunderstorms are dangerous to boaters. When thunder is heard, lightning is close by. On a lake, a person in a boat is the highest point for a large distance in any direction. A boater can become a lightning rod. The best thing for boaters to do is to get to shore and get out of the water. Once the threat passes, it will be safe for them to boat again.

or passengers. A boater should never stand up in the boat.

When on a river, boaters need to keep the craft under control. Even a gentle current can overpower an adult. Boaters should be aware if the speed of the water increases. Boating is not like hiking or cycling. When boaters come across something that is beyond their skill level, they can't just turn back the way they came. It is helpful to practice capsizing. This should be done in a safe environment, with plenty of rescuers around. Fears will be conquered, and people can learn what to do in an emergency.

RAFTING SAFETY

Rafts don't have brakes. The river never stops flowing. It is important for boaters to keep their eyes downstream. They need to plan their moves in advance. Having basic safety equipment and a good dose of common sense will help everyone have an enjoyable adventure.

All boaters should be prepared to capsize and know how to recover from it.

In addition to PFDs, a rafter's best friend is a helmet. Helmets save heads from hazards both on the boat and in the river. Rafts should be outfitted with rescue equipment. The outside line or grab rope

Helmets and PFDs are crucial safety gear for rafters.

is attached to the boat. Rafters who are thrown into the water can hang on to the line until a fellow rafter helps them back in. Rafters should carry a throw bag. This is a rescue device with a rope attached to it. It can be thrown to overboard rafters and used to tow them back in.

Rafting is best done with a professional white-water outfitter. These businesses provide certified guides and use quality equipment. All rafters should pay close attention to the safety lecture provided. Most importantly, the lecture will give tips on how rafters can rescue themselves or others in the event that

Rafters should always listen to their guide and follow his or her instructions.

someone goes overboard. Once they are on the river, it is critical for rafters to listen to the guide. He or she will tell when it's time to lean left or right, to paddle, or to stop paddling.

A white-water paddle is necessary to steer the boat. But it can also become a safety hazard in rough waters if it's not held properly. One hand should be at the base of the shaft, above the blade. The other must be on the end of the shaft over the T-grip. This handle is made of hard plastic. It can knock out teeth and blacken eyes. Keeping a hand over the grip can soften the blow if the paddle accidentally hits another rafter.

As the ride gets wilder, rafters can get thrown out of the boat. Most rivers have major safety hazards called strainers. These are rocks or large tree limbs hidden under the water. Strainers let the water flow through, but a person will get stuck in them. A paddler can get sucked under the water and drown. If paddlers find themselves in the river, they should pick up their feet, relax, and let the current carry them to shore.

CHAPTER 5

RESPECT THE ENVIRONMENT

Whether it's a peaceful day on the lake or a wild ride through the rapids, boating is a unique way to interact with nature. But boating can have negative impacts on the environment. Boaters need to respect the water and surrounding areas.

LITTERING IS UNLAWFUL

Approximately 20 percent of litter in the water comes from offshore. Some debris does not break down and stays in the environment for a long time. Balloons, plastic bags, and fishing gear last for centuries. Plastic bottles and six-pack rings remain

Boaters must discard their trash properly.

Toxins in the water can be passed along to humans who eat fish.

for over 400 years. Over time, this trash builds up, having a devastating impact on water quality and wildlife habitats.

Dumping garbage from boats can cause wildlife to become trapped. Mammals, turtles, birds, and fish can die when they are caught in the trash. Researchers think this problem has caused populations of some marine animals to decrease. Nonfatal injuries can also be serious. They can cause breathing or swimming difficulties. Injuries can get in the way of feeding or raising young properly. It is a federal crime to throw plastic into the water. Boaters should tie down all solid waste and stow it until it can be properly disposed of on land.

KEEPING TOXINS OUT

Chemicals used to clean and protect boats can seep into the water. Toxins that endanger aquatic life are also dangerous to humans. They can be swallowed or absorbed through the skin while swimming. Detergents and paints can cause cancer, birth defects, and even death. Boaters should

TOXIC FISH

Many waterways used for boating are also used for catching fish or other foods. Toxins that endanger marine life also threaten humans. Chemicals in the water are absorbed by the fish. Eating this contaminated food can cause health problems such as birth defects and cancer.

use paints that are environmentally safe. Boats can be cleaned with natural, nontoxic solutions. A boater's safest option for preventing pollution is storing the vessel on land when it is not being used.

Human waste in water is a major concern. All toilet activity should be done at least 200 feet (60 m) from any body of water. The discharge of waste from boats can cause high bacteria and virus counts. Humans can develop serious diseases such as gastroenteritis, hepatitis, and cholera if the contaminated water enters their bodies.

INVASIVE SPECIES

Aquatic invasive species are plants and animals that are not native to a habitat. These organisms do not have natural predators in their new environments. That allows them to spread and cause damage to native species. Many invasive species attach themselves to boats. As the vessels travel from one body of water to another, the invasive species travel with them. The invasive species introduce new parasites or disrupt the food supply in the habitat.

Boaters should clean their boats before they leave the area. They should remove plants and animals and dispose of them on land. Rinsing the boat and letting

All boaters should clean their craft to prevent the spread of toxins and invasive species.

it dry before entering another body of water will help prevent spreading invasive species. By being aware of their impacts, boaters can help keep marine environments safe and unspoiled.

Boating is a recreational activity that people of all ages can enjoy. From a peaceful canoe trip across a placid lake at dawn to the rush of an exhilarating raft ride down a rushing river, boating offers many different ways to enjoy a day on the water.

GLOSSARY

capsize
Turn over so that the bottom is on top.

contaminated
Made dirty or dangerous by adding something harmful.

indigenous
Living naturally in a certain area or environment.

invasive
Tending to spread in a harmful way.

parallel
Running in the same direction, an equal distance apart.

parasites
Organisms that live in or on another organism and get food or protection from it.

pivot
The action of turning around a single point.

precaution
Something that is done to prevent trouble in the future.

propulsion
The act of making something move.

strenuous
Requiring great effort and energy.

synchronize
To make things happen at the same time and speed.

yacht
A large boat that is used for racing or pleasure.

MORE INFORMATION

BOOKS

Brown, Daniel James. *The Boys in the Boat: The True Story of an American Team's Epic Journey to Win Gold at the 1936 Olympics: Young Readers Adaptation*. New York: Puffin, 2016.

Rooney, Anne. *The Science of Seafaring: The Float-tastic Facts about Ships*. New York: Franklin Watts, 2019.

Volant, Iris. *Boats: Fast & Slow*. New York: Flying Eye Books, 2018.

ONLINE RESOURCES

Booklinks
NONFICTION NETWORK
FREE! ONLINE NONFICTION RESOURCES

To learn more about boating, please visit **abdobooklinks.com** or scan this QR code. These links are routinely monitored and updated to provide the most current information available.

INDEX

boating
    demographics, 9
    history, 7–9
    terminology, 10

canoeing, 13, 18–24
capsizing, 34, 39
Charles II (English
    king), 9
clothing, 16

gear, 17, 30–31, 33, 36

helmets, 35
history of boating,
    7–9

International Scale of
    River Difficulty, 15
invasive species,
    44–45

kayaking, 13–14,
    20–22, 24–26

litter, 40–43

oars, 13, 18–23

paddles, 13–15,
    18–21, 23–27, 39
personal flotation
    devices (PFDs),
    28–30, 35

rowing, 10–13, 18,
    21–23, 24

safety, 28–37

toxins, 43–44

water traffic rules,
    32–33
weather, 31, 33
white-water rafting,
    4–6, 15–16, 20, 27,
    34 39

yacht clubs, 7

ABOUT THE AUTHOR

Patricia Hutchison is a former teacher who has written dozens of nonfiction children's books about science, nature, history, and geography. She lives in South Carolina with her husband. They love to travel throughout the United States and to other countries.